Teen Stress Workbook

Facilitator Reproducible
Self-Assessments, Exercises
& Educational Handouts

**Ester A. Leutenberg
& John J. Liptak, EdD**

Illustrated by
Amy L. Brodsky, LISW-S

wholeperson
Stress & Wellness Publishers
Duluth, Minnesota

Whole Person
101 W. 2nd St., Suite 203
Duluth MN 55802

800-247-6789

books@wholeperson.com
www.wholeperson.com

Teen Stress Workbook
Facilitator Reproducible Self-Assessments,
Exercises & Educational Handouts

Printed in the United States of America

10 9 8 7 6 5 4 3 2 1

Editorial Director: Carlene Sippola
Art Director: Joy Morgan Dey

Library of Congress Control Number: 2011938511
ISBN: 978-1-57025-258-7

Using This Book *(For the professional)*

Adolescence can be a period of significant change for most teens, leading them to experience stress.

Stress is the way our bodies and minds react to changes in life. Stress, an uncomfortable feeling teens get, is triggered when they are overwhelmed, out of control, frustrated, or excessively worried about something.

Because of the multiple life changes teens must work through, many find themselves under more stress than they have formerly experienced in their life.

Stress can come from many different sources:

- Family members' constant reminders such as "Don't use drugs," "Go out for that team," "I don't like your friends," "Make new friends," "Get good grades," "You have a curfew," and "Stay out of trouble."

- Friends frequent reminders and suggestions such as "Be cool," "Skip that class," "Take one drink," "Try this," "Don't hang around that person," "Let's pick on that person," and "Let's cheat on the test."

- Teen inner thoughts and worries such as "I need to lose weight," "If I don't do better I will never get into college," "My parents will be upset with me," "I don't fit in at school," and "I should get a job."

- Adults' remarks such as "You need to get that done," "You were late," and "Get it done or you will get into trouble."

No one can avoid stress. Small amounts of stress can be okay, but chronic stress can push people beyond the limits of what can be handled.

Some facts about stress:

- Teens are trying to cope with many physical, social, and emotional changes during adolescence.

- Teens are struggling to make their own decisions and develop their own identity.

- Teens are more resilient than most people expect.

- Teens need to feel competent and in control in order to cope with stress.

- Teens often have trouble identifying or expressing their feelings about being stressed.

- Teens are struggling for independence from their family.

- Teens are torn between their need for more responsibility and their dependence on family members and adults.

- When teens are experiencing chronic stress, even the smallest amount of additional stress can trigger strong negative emotional responses.

(Continued on the next page)

Using This Book *(For the professional, continued)*

The *Teen Stress Workbook* contains five separate sections to help teens learn more about themselves and the skills they possess and learn to manage the stress that occurs in their lives. Participants will learn new skills and the importance of preventing, managing and coping with stress and its symptoms.

- **How Do I know When I'm Stressed Scale** helps teens to explore the behavioral, emotional, and physical signs and symptoms, and their intensity.

- **My Stressors Scale** helps teens examine the various sources of stress in their lives.

- **Eustress vs. Distress Scale** helps teens identify ways to build resiliency in preventing and dealing with stress and its symptoms.

- **Stressed for Success Scale** helps teens identify the various ways that they put too much pressure on themselves.

- **How I Deal with My Stress Scale** helps teens identify their effectiveness in coping with stress and the symptoms of stress.

Use Codes for Confidentiality

Confidentiality is a term for any action that preserves the privacy of other people. Because teens completing the activities in this workbook might be asked to answer assessment items and to journal about and explore their relationships, you will need to discuss confidentiality before you begin using the materials in this workbook. Maintaining confidentiality is important because it shows respect for others and allows participants to explore their feelings without hurting anyone's feelings or fearing gossip, harm or retribution.

In order to maintain confidentiality, explain to the participants that they need to assign a **name code for each person or each group of people** they write about as they complete the various activities in the workbook. For example, a friend named Joey who enjoys going to hockey games might be titled JLHG (Joey Loves Hockey Games) for a particular exercise. In order to protect their friends' identities, they should not use actual names or initials of people or groups, only name codes.

(Continued on the next page)

Using This Book *(For the professional, continued)*

The *Teen Stress Workbook* is designed to be used either independently or as part of an integrated curriculum. You may administer one of the assessments and the journaling exercises to an individual or a group with whom you are working, or you may administer a number of the assessments over one or more days.

This book includes the following reproducible pages in the first five sections:

- **Assessment Instruments** – Self-assessment inventories with scoring directions and interpretation materials. Group facilitators can choose one or more of the activities relevant to their participants.

- **Activity Handouts** – Practical questions and activities that prompt self-reflection and promote self-understanding. These questions and activities foster introspection and promote pro-social behaviors.

- **Quotations** – Quotations are used in each section to provide insight and promote reflection. Participants will be asked to select one or more of the quotations and journal about what the quotations mean to them.

- **Reflective Questions for Journaling** – Self-exploration activities and journaling exercises specific to each assessment to enhance self-discovery, learning, and healing.

- **Educational Handouts** – Handouts designed to enhance instruction can be used by individuals or in groups to promote a positive understanding of managing stress. They can be distributed, scanned and converted into masters for overheads or transparencies, projected or written on boards and/or discussed.

Who Should Use This Program?

This book has been designed as a practical tool to help professionals such as therapists, counselors, psychologists, teachers, group leaders, etc. Depending on the role of the professional using the *Teen Stress Workbook* and the specific person's or group's needs, these sections can be used individually or combined for a more comprehensive approach.

Why Use Self-Assessments?

- Self-assessments are important in teaching various stress management skills because they help participants to engage in several ways:

- Become aware of the primary motivators that guide their behavior

- Explore and let go of troublesome habits and behavioral patterns learned in childhood

- Examine the effects of unconscious childhood messages

- Gain insight and recognize a "wake-up call" for behavioral change

- Focus thinking on behavioral goals for positive change

- Uncover personal resources that can help them to cope better with problems and difficulties

- Explore personal characteristics without judgment

- Identify personal strengths and weaknesses

Because the assessments are presented in a straightforward and easy-to-use format, individuals can self-administer, score and interpret each assessment at their own pace.

About the Assessments, Journaling Activities and Educational Handouts

Materials in the Assessments, Journaling Activities, and Educational Handouts sections in this book are reproducible and can be photocopied for participants' use. Assessments contained in this book focus on self-reported data and thus are similar to ones used by psychologists, counselors, therapists, and career consultants. The accuracy and usefulness of the information provided is dependent on the truthful information that each participant provides. By being honest, participants help themselves to learn about unproductive and ineffective patterns in their lives, and to uncover information that might be keeping them from being as happy or as successful as they might be.

An assessment instrument can provide participants with valuable information about themselves; however, these assessments cannot measure or identify everything. The assessments' purpose is not to pigeonhole certain characteristics, but rather to allow participants to consider all of their characteristics. This book contains self-assessments, not tests. Tests measure knowledge or whether something is right or wrong. For the assessments in this book, there are no right or wrong answers. These assessments ask for personal opinions or attitudes about a topic of importance in the participant's life.

When administering the assessments in this workbook, remember that the items are generically written so that they will be applicable to a wide variety of people but may not account for every possible variable for every person. No assessments are specifically tailored to one person. Assessments are structured to help a variety of participants to identify negative themes in their lives and find ways to break the hold of these patterns and their effects.

Advise teen participants taking the assessments that they should not spend too much time trying to analyze the content of the questions; they should think about the questions in general and then spontaneously report how they feel about each one. Whatever the results of the assessment, encourage participants to talk about their findings and their feelings pertaining to what have they discovered about themselves. Talking about issues such as teen stress and coping can be therapeutic and beneficial.

The *Teen Stress Workbook* sections serve as an avenue for individual self-reflection, as well as group experiences revolving around identified topics of importance. Each assessment includes directions for easy administration, scoring and interpretation. In addition, each section includes exploratory activities, reflective journaling activities, insightful quotations and educational handouts to help participants to learn more about the stress they are experiencing and how to effectively manage the stress they will inevitably have in the future.

(Continued on the next page)

About the Assessments, Journaling Activities and Educational Handouts *(Continued)*

The art of self-reflection goes back many centuries and is rooted in many of the world's greatest spiritual and philosophical traditions. Socrates, the ancient Greek philosopher, was known to walk the streets engaging the people he met in philosophical reflection and dialogue. He felt that this type of activity was so important in life that he proclaimed, "The unexamined life is not worth living!" The unexamined life is one in which the same routine is continually repeated without ever thinking about its meaning to one's life and how this life really could be lived. However, a structured reflection and examination of beliefs, assumptions, characteristics and patterns can provide a better understanding which can lead to a more satisfying life and career. A greater level of self-understanding about important life skills is often necessary to make positive, self-directed changes in repetitive negative patterns throughout life. The assessments and exercises in this book can help promote this self-understanding. Through involvement with the in-depth activities, each participant claims ownership in the development of positive patterns.

Journaling is an extremely powerful tool for enhancing self-discovery, learning, transcending traditional problems, breaking ineffective life and career habits, and helping people to heal from psychological traumas of the past. From a physical point of view, writing reduces stress and lowers muscle tension, blood pressure and heart rate levels. Psychologically, writing reduces feelings of sadness, depression and general anxiety, and it leads to a greater level of life satisfaction and optimism. Behaviorally, writing leads to enhanced social skills, emotional intelligence and creativity.

By combining reflective assessment and journaling, your participants will engage in a powerful method for managing the inevitable stress they will have in the future.

Thanks to the following professionals whose input in this book has been invaluable!

Amy Brodsky, LISW-S
Carol Butler, MS Ed, RN, C
Kathy Khalsa, MAJS, OTR / L

Jay Leutenberg
Hannah Lavoie
Kathy Liptak, Ed.D.

Eileen Regen, M.Ed., CJE

Introduction for the Participant

Like adults, you experience stress every day. You will benefit from learning effective stress management skills. A little bit of stress is okay, and can even be helpful. However, when you become overloaded with stress or the stress lasts for long periods of time, the stress needs to be managed. When you are unable to adequately manage your stress, you may feel anxiety or depression, experience physical problems, withdraw from family and friends, display aggression or bullying behavior and even become involved with drug and/or alcohol abuse.

You will experience stress when you perceive a situation too challenging, too difficult, too painful, or beyond your control. Some of your stress sources might include the following:

- Changes in your physical appearance
- Negative feelings about yourself
- Problems with peers at school
- Unsafe living conditions at home
- Separation or divorce of parents
- Death of a loved one

- Death of a pet
- Change in family living situation
- Move to a new neighborhood or city
- Change of schools
- Peer pressure
- Bullying

This workbook will help you develop and polish the skills you need to build basic resiliency habits, prime your coping skills when you encounter stress, and manage effective stress management skills. You may encounter many of the above types of stress in your lifetime. When you encounter negative changes in your environment, changes occur in your mind and body to prepare you for that change. You can, however, minimize and reverse this stress response by using the stress management techniques contained in this workbook.

You will be encouraged throughout this workbook to complete assessments, journaling activities and exercises. Because active involvement is as important as talking about theories, it is to your best advantage to take the time to complete all of the skill-building exercises.

The *Teen Stress Workbook* is designed to help you learn more about yourself, identify the primary reasons you are feeling stress, and find better ways to use your newfound stress management skills to feel more confident and less helpless, and to cope and make better choices when responding to stress.

IMPORTANT

You will be asked to respond to assessment items and to journal about and explore your relationships with your friends. Everyone has the right to confidentiality, and you need to honor the right to privacy of others. Think about it this way – you would not want someone writing things about you that other people could read about. Your friends feel this way also.

In order to maintain the confidentiality of your friends, assign people code names based on things you know about them. For example, a friend named Sherry who loves to wear purple might be coded as SWP (Sherry Wears Purple). Do not use actual names of people or groups when you are listing your friends.

Teen Stress Workbook
TABLE OF CONTENTS

TABLE OF CONTENTS

TABLE OF CONTENTS

How Do I Know When I'm Stressed? Scale

Name_____

Date_____

How Do I Know When I'm Stressed? Scale Directions

We all experience stress, but we all react to each stress differently. Signs and symptoms differ from person to person. Some react to stress behaviorally, while others react emotionally or physically. This assessment will help you learn more about how you experience stress so that you will know when you are experiencing too much stress in your life.

This assessment contains descriptors of the symptoms of stress that are divided into three sections. Think about the times when you were or are feeling stressed. Place a check in the boxes that describe your reactions to the stress. In the following example, the ✔ shows that the person completing the assessment forgets things and feels bored when experiencing stress.

When I am stressed, I find myself... (✔)

- ❑ Fighting a lot
- ❑ Forgetting things
- ☑ Feeling bored
- ☑ Writing sad e-mail/texts

This is not a test and there are no right or wrong answers. Do not spend too much time thinking about your answers. Your initial response will be the most true for you.
Be sure to respond to every statement.

(Turn to the next page and begin)

How Do I Know When I'm Stressed? Scale

When I am stressed, I find myself... (✔)

- ❏ Fighting a lot
- ❏ Forgetting things
- ❏ Feeling bored
- ❏ Writing sad e-mails/texts
- ❏ Isolating myself
- ❏ Drinking alcoholic beverages
- ❏ Taking illegal/addictive drugs
- ❏ Getting poor grades
- ❏ Focusing poorly
- ❏ Losing my temper easily
- ❏ Avoiding my studies
- ❏ Getting overwhelmed easily
- ❏ Drawing sad pictures
- ❏ Bullying others
- ❏ Failing to cope
- ❏ Cursing
- ❏ Being bullied
- ❏ Wanting to run away from things
- ❏ Letting little things bother me
- ❏ Verbally attacking others
- ❏ Other_____
- ❏ Other_____

- ❏ Feeling anxious
- ❏ Feeling upset
- ❏ Feeling depressed
- ❏ Feeling sad
- ❏ Feeling hopeless
- ❏ Feeling bad about myself
- ❏ Losing my self-confidence
- ❏ Feeling out of control
- ❏ Getting distracted easily
- ❏ Feeling tired constantly
- ❏ Feeling like I don't care
- ❏ Worrying
- ❏ Being pessimistic a lot
- ❏ Feeling abandoned
- ❏ Feeling fearful
- ❏ Feeling grouchy
- ❏ Having aches and pains
- ❏ Feeling picked on
- ❏ Crying often
- ❏ Feeling alone
- ❏ Other _____
- ❏ Other _____

B TOTAL = _____   **E TOTAL = _____**

(Continued on the next page)

How Do I Know When I'm Stressed?
Scale (continued)

When I am stressed, I find myself... (✔)

❑ Skipping meals

❑ Sleeping too much

❑ Experiencing a fast heartbeat

❑ Perspiring a lot

❑ Having clammy hands

❑ Acting without thinking

❑ Having nightmares

❑ Biting my fingernails

❑ Pulling my hair out

❑ Sleeping restlessly

❑ Getting an upset stomach

❑ Losing weight rapidly

❑ Eating constantly

❑ Getting a rash

❑ Suffering from headaches

❑ Feeling dizzy or light-headed

❑ Feeling bad all over

❑ Feeling tired all the time

❑ Crying a lot

❑ Feeling my heart racing or thumping

❑ Other_____

❑ Other_____

P TOTAL = _____

(Go to the Scoring Directions on the next page)

How Do I Know When I'm Stressed? Scale
Scoring Directions

Everyone experiences signs and symptoms of stress. It is important to identify your symptoms when you are stressed, to become aware of them and to notice how you are affected. This assessment will help you explore the various ways you experience symptoms of stress. For each of the sections, count the number of boxes in which you placed a ✔. You will receive a score from 0 to 22. Put that total on the line marked TOTAL at the end of each section.

Transfer your totals to the spaces below:

B (BEHAVIORAL) TOTAL = _____

E (EMOTIONAL) TOTAL = _____

P (PHYSICAL) TOTAL = _____

Profile Interpretation

Individual Scales Scores	Result	Indications
15 to 22	high	If you score high on any of the scales, you tend to experience a great deal of stress in that mode.
8 to 14	moderate	If you score moderate on any of the scales, you tend to experience some stress in that mode..
0 to 7	low	If you score low on any of the scales, you tend to not experience much stress in that mode.

For scales which you scored in the **Moderate** or **High** range, find the descriptions on the pages that follow. Then, read the description and complete the exercises that are included. No matter how you scored, low, moderate or high, you will benefit from these exercises.

Behavioral Coping Skills – Mental Imagery

Ignoring problems that cause you stress will not make the problems go away. In fact they probably will get worse. You can build skills in several ways so that when you encounter stress, you can cope with it. These coping skills can be behavioral, emotional, or physical.

What immediate types of things can you do to reduce the stress (Avoid certain people, do certain things, avoid places, etc.)?

_____

_____

Stop worrying needlessly. What could you stop worrying about?

_____

_____

Let go of things you cannot control. What might those be?

_____

_____

Learn to relax. Working with images can be a useful way to reduce anxiety. Mental Imagery is the use of memories of visual events to project a mental picture in your mind. Many different forms of mental imagery exist. Here is an example:

I picture myself on my favorite beach. When I begin to feel stress I can project myself to this beach. I just close my eyes and picture myself walking on the sand. I love the feel of the sand beneath my feet. I imagine walking close to the water. The sand feels cooler there. I smell the fresh scent of the ocean. I feel the warm air blowing through my hair. With each breath I take I imagine breathing in the beautiful, vivid colors that are present. This is my personal paradise.

Now, you do the same. You write out a pleasant imagery scene, one that you will like picturing and remembering. Include what your senses will experience – what you smell, hear and feel. When you find yourself in an anxiety-producing situation, you can begin to imagine this scene vividly.

_____

_____

_____

Behavioral Coping Skills – Total-Body Relaxation

Total-Body Relaxation, often called Progressive Muscle Relaxation, is a simple technique used to stop anxiety and relax the tension in your body by relaxing all of the muscles throughout your body one group at a time.

Read through the following script several times before you attempt to do the Total-Body Relaxation.

> *Take a few deep breaths, and begin to relax.*
>
> *Imagine a box and put all of your worries inside. Close the box.*
>
> *Let each part of your body begin to relax ... starting with your feet.*
>
> *Imagine your feet relaxing as all of your tension begins to fade away.*
>
> *Imagine the relaxation moving up into your calves and thighs ...
>   feel them begin to relax.*
>
> *Allow the relaxation to move into your waist.*
>
> *Your entire body from the waist down is now completely relaxed.*
>
> *Continue now to let the relaxation move into your hips and stomach.*
>
> *Let go of any strain and discomfort you might feel.*
>
> *Allow the relaxation to move into your chest
>   until your chest feels completely relaxed.*
>
> *Just enjoy the feeling of complete relaxation.*
>
> *Continue to let the relaxation move through the muscles of your shoulders,
>   then spread down into your upper arms, into your elbows, and finally all the way
>   down to your wrists and hands.*
>
> *Put aside all of your worries.*
>
> *Let yourself be totally present in the moment and let yourself relax more and more.
>   Let all the muscles in your neck unwind and let the relaxation move into your chin
>   and jaws.*
>
> *Feel the tension around your eyes flow away as the relaxation moves
>   throughout your face and head.*
>
> *Feel your forehead relax and your entire head beginning to feel lighter.*
>
> *Let yourself drift deeper and deeper into relaxation and peace.*

Read the above paragraph several times or read the script calmly, aloud in a tape recorder and then playback to hear your own voice, giving yourself instructions. Find a quiet location where you can practice Total-Body Relaxation. Assume a comfortable position in a chair. Take off your jewelry and glasses so that you are totally free. Try to let the relaxation happen without having to force it. If during the relaxation you lose concentration, don't be concerned, just begin again.

Behavioral Coping Skills–Breathing

Breathing is one of the best ways for you to allow your mind and body to experience feelings of deep relaxation. You can do this by spreading relaxing thoughts through your body from head to foot. When you are relaxed, you breathe fully and deeply, from your abdomen. It is virtually impossible to be tense and breathe from your abdomen. Abdominal breathing triggers a relaxation response in you. The following exercise will help you experience this relaxation.

Before you begin, you should get as comfortable as you possibly can. Mentally begin to clear your mind of the busy thoughts that keep running through it. Start to relax. Breath through your nose, taking a deep breath, and then open your mouth slightly and let the air slowly slip out. Try this breathing now!

Take a deep breath. As you breath out, silently say "Relax and let go of my stress." Inhale slowly through your nose, down deep as possible into your lungs. You should see your abdomen rise. When you have taken a full breath, pause for a moment and then exhale slowly through your mouth. Be sure to exhale thoroughly. Try this now.

Feel yourself relaxing even further. The more you can let go, the more relaxed you will become. You will notice that as you relax more and more, your breathing will become slower. Feel all of the tension leaving your body and being replaced by well-being. Take ten of these full abdominal breaths. Keep your breaths as smooth and regular as possible. As you continue this process, you can try slowing down the rate at which you take breaths. Pause for a second after each breath you take. Try this now.

Let this relaxation now enter other parts of your body through your deep breaths. Keep your eyes closed gently. Relax your face, head, and neck. As you continue your deep breathing, think about each part of your body relaxing, you will feel the tension totally leaving your body. You will begin to feel peaceful, calm, and refreshed. Allow this relaxation to spread to your shoulders, and then your arms. Allow the relaxation to spread to your chest and stomach, then your hips and legs. Feel the relaxation spread into your feet. You are now totally relaxed. Try this now.

Physical Coping Skills – Eat Better

You can build your stress-coping resources by eating well. Good nutrition makes a big difference in your health and how well you will deal with stress. Following are some healthy eating habits you might need to adopt.

Eating Habits	What I Eat Now	How I Can Eat Better
Good Breakfast		
3 Meals a Day		
6-8 Glasses of Water a Day		
Healthy Foods		
Healthy Drinks		
Vegetables		
Fruit		
Healthy Snacks/Treats		
Other		

What stops you from making these improvements?

_____

_____

What can you do about that?

_____

_____

Physical Coping Skills–Sleep Better

You can build your stress coping resources by eating well. Good nutrition makes a big difference in your health and how well you will deal with stress. Following are some bedtime habits you might explore to determine why you are not sleeping well.

Bedtime Habits	What I Do Now	How I Can Sleep Better
Texting in Bed		
Reading in Bed		
Talking with Friends		
Worrying about the next day		
Watching television		
Eating before bed		
Playing video games in bed		
Other		

What stops you from making these improvements?

_____

_____

What can you do about that?

_____

_____

Emotional Coping Skills – Creativity

When you are engrossed in creative activities, you will stop thinking about your stressful situations. Activities can help you release pent up emotions and feel better about yourself. Check the ways you can express your emotions through creative activities and write specifics on the line attached.

❑ Acting _____

❑ Blogging _____

❑ Building models, woodworking, etc. _____

❑ Crafting unique items _____

❑ Creating computer program _____

❑ Dancing _____

❑ Designing a web page _____

❑ Doodling _____

❑ Drawing _____

❑ Finding ways to help others _____

❑ Making origami _____

❑ Making video biography of older person _____

❑ Painting _____

❑ Painting / Sketching / Drawing _____

❑ Playing a musical instrument _____

❑ Playing an instrument in a band or orchestra _____

❑ Pottery / Ceramics _____

❑ Quilting _____

❑ Rapping _____

❑ Scrapbooking _____

❑ Sculpting _____

❑ Singing _____

❑ Singing in a choir _____

❑ Starting a band _____

❑ Taking pictures _____

❑ Visiting museums _____

❑ Writing poems _____

❑ Writing stories or articles _____

❑ Other _____

Emotional Coping Skills – Talk with Others and Identifying Passions

Talk with Others

Think about the adults in your life whom you trust and would feel comfortable talking to. Who are these adults? Use name codes.

_____

_____

_____

Identify Your Passions

You can reduce stress by engaging in activities you enjoy.
What would your top five activities be?

Five Activities I Enjoy	How They Might Reduce My Stress
Ex: Martial Arts	It is good exercise that helps me focus on the present.
1.	
2.	
3.	
4.	
5.	

Emotional Coping Skills – Laughing or Crying

You can begin to truly feel your emotions by either laughing or crying or both. In the top table, write about ways that you could laugh more. In the bottom table, write about the ways that you could begin to cry if that's what you need.

Ways I Could Laugh More
Ex: Buy a one-a-day joke calendar

Ways I Could Cry If I Need To
Ex: Watch a sad movie

Emotional Coping Skills – Help Others

Helping others is a good way to regulate the stress you are experiencing. This can include many different forms of volunteering such as walking animals at the local humane society, helping build houses for Habitat for Humanity, reading to seniors, etc. What types of volunteering might you like to get involved with? Complete the following chart to explore your helping interests:

Agency/Facility	What I Could Offer to Do	How It Would Help Others
Ex: Food Kitchen	*Sort the cans and boxes*	*People will get a good variety of foods*

Stress Management Skills

Write about the Behavioral Stress Management techniques you like best.

Mental Imagery, Total Body Relaxation and Breathing

_____

_____

_____

_____

_____

_____

_____

Write about the Physical Stress Management techniques you like best.

Eat Better, Sleep Better and Exercise

_____

_____

_____

_____

_____

_____

_____

Write about the Emotional Stress Management techniques you like best.

Creativity, Talk with Others, Passions, Laugh, Cry, Helping Others

_____

_____

_____

_____

_____

_____

_____

Stress Management Quotations

Choose two of the quotes below. How does each speak to you about your stress? Perhaps you will find a quote that you disagree with. Write about that also.

❏ *It is not stress that kills us, it is our reaction to it.*　　**~ Hans Selye**

❏ *There must be quite a few things that a hot bath won't cure, but I don't know many of them.*

　　　　　　　　　　　　　　　　　　　　　　　　　~ Sylvia Plath

❏ *Stress is like an iceberg. We can see one-eighth of it above, but what about what's below?*

　　　　　　　　　　　　　　　　　　　　　　　~ Author Unknown

_____

_____

_____

_____

_____

_____

_____

_____

_____

_____

_____

_____

_____

_____

_____

_____

_____

_____

_____

_____

_____

Reactions to Too Much Stress

- Overdoing activities such as sports, music, clubs

- Disruptive behaviors

- Poor grades in school

- Prolonged absences in school

- Sleeping too much

- Sleeping restlessly, fitfully

- Overeating

- Eating too little

- Eating unhealthy foods

- Lacking focus

- Spending less time with good, trusted friends

- Spending too much time with risk-taking friends

Additional Ways of Coping with Stress

- Talking to a trusted friend or adult
- Putting aside negative self-talk
- Journaling about your stressors
- Improving your problem-solving skills
- Managing your time wisely
- Considering options carefully when making a decision
- Looking to your faith and spirituality
- Developing a network of supportive friends and family
- Feeling good about a good enough job rather than perfection
- Learning from your mistakes
- Rehearsing and practicing positive behaviors in difficult situations
- Developing assertive skills
- Learning coping skills
- Avoiding caffeine intake
- Feeling proud of your accomplishments
- Exercising daily
- Avoiding illegal drugs, alcohol and tobacco

SECTION II:
My Stressors Scale

Name_____

Date_____

My Stressors Scale
Directions

You experience stress from a wide variety of sources:

- School

- Your family

- Your personal life

- Your social life

This assessment is divided into four sections and contains descriptors of the types of stress you may be experiencing, or have recently experienced. Place a check in the boxes that describe stress you have recently experienced or are currently experiencing. The example below shows that the person completing the assessment has experienced stress in school by taking hard classes.

Types of stress I have experienced or am experiencing now:

SCHOOL
- ❑ Poor grades
- ☑ Hard classes
- ❑ Being bullied

This is not a test and there are no right or wrong answers. Do not spend too much time thinking about your answers. Your initial response will be the most true for you. Be sure to respond to every statement.

(Turn to the next page and begin)

My Stressors Scale

Types of stress I have experienced or am experiencing now:

SCHOOL

- ❏ Poor grades
- ❏ Hard classes
- ❏ Being bullied
- ❏ Peer pressure
- ❏ What to do after graduation
- ❏ Decisions about working
- ❏ Taking tests
- ❏ Taking on too many activities
- ❏ Teachers
- ❏ Problems with friends or lack of them
- ❏ Demands of school work
- ❏ Meeting deadlines
- ❏ Too high expectations
- ❏ Problems studying
- ❏ No time to volunteer or help someone
- ❏ Suspension from school
- ❏ Other _____
- ❏ Other _____

FAMILY

- ❏ Blended family issues
- ❏ Parents arguing a lot
- ❏ Loss of a family member
- ❏ Issues with step-parents
- ❏ Arguing with brothers/sisters
- ❏ Alcoholic parent(s)
- ❏ Addicted parent(s)
- ❏ Parents' divorce
- ❏ Parents' separation
- ❏ Illness of a family member
- ❏ Financial problems
- ❏ Unsafe living environment
- ❏ Birth of a sibling
- ❏ Loss of job by parent or guardian
- ❏ Family member in jail
- ❏ Issues with step-parent or step-siblings
- ❏ Other_____
- ❏ Other_____

☑ **SCHOOL TOTAL = _____**   ☑ **FAMILY TOTAL = _____**

(Continued on the next page)

     © 2012 WHOLE PERSON ASSOCIATES, 101 W. 2nd ST., SUITE 203, DULUTH MN 55802 • 800-247-6789

(My Stressors Scale continued)

Type of stress I have experienced or am experiencing now:

PERSONAL	SOCIAL
❏ Negative feelings about myself	❏ Break up
❏ Changes in my body	❏ Loss of a pet
❏ Expect too much	❏ Loss of a friend
❏ In trouble with the police	❏ Move to a new town
❏ Changing schools	❏ No friends
❏ Moving to a new neighborhood	❏ Not fitting in socially
❏ Taking a job	❏ Pressure to take drugs
❏ Competing in sports	❏ Pressure to drink alcohol
❏ Fighting or bullying	❏ Pressure to have sex
❏ Concern about weight	❏ Pressure to dress differently
❏ Eating disorder	❏ Pressure to join a gang
❏ Pregnancy	❏ Dating
❏ Physical appearance	❏ Gender identity
❏ Having an addiction	❏ Got married
❏ Struggling with an illness or disability	❏ Pregnancy in my relationship
❏ Ran away from home	❏ Not getting into a club or sport
❏ Other _____	❏ Other_____
❏ Other _____	❏ Other_____

☑ **PERSONAL TOTAL = _____**   ☑ **SOCIAL TOTAL = _____**

(Go to the Scoring Directions on the next page)

My Stressors Scale
Scoring Directions

Because stress is part of life, it is hard to avoid it. The first step in managing stress is to identify the aspects of your life in which you are experiencing a lot of stress, become aware of it and notice how it affects you. This assessment will help you explore the various ways you are experiencing stress in your life. For each of the sections, count the number of boxes in which you placed a check. You will receive a score from 0 to 18. Put that total on the line marked TOTAL at the end of each section.

Transfer your totals to the spaces below:

_____ = **SCHOOL TOTAL**

_____ = **FAMILY TOTAL**

_____ = **PERSONAL TOTAL**

_____ = **SOCIAL TOTAL**

Profile Interpretation

Individual Scales Scores	Result	Indications
13 to 18	high	If you score high on any of the scales, you have experienced in the past, or are presently experiencing, a great many stressors.
7 to 12	moderate	If you score moderate on any of the scales, you have experienced in the past, or are presently experiencing, significant stressors.
0 to 6	low	If you score low on any of the scales, you have not experienced in the past, or are not presently experiencing, many stressors.

No matter how you scored, low, moderate or high, you will benefit from the exercises that follow.

School

People scoring high on this scale tend to experience stress related to school. This stress may be related to your grades, participating in too many activities, your choice of friends or lack of friends, being bullied, having too high expectations, and relationships with teachers. The following exercises are designed to help you explore the pressures you experience related to school.

How do you feel about the grades you earn?

_____

_____

_____

_____

Who puts the most pressure on you about school? Use name codes.

_____

_____

_____

_____

Why do you think these people are pressuring you?

_____

_____

_____

_____

Is it under your control to change this? If so, what could you do?

_____

_____

_____

_____

School Pressure

Complete this chart to identify your pressures at school. (Use name codes.)

Type of Pressure	Who Is Putting This Pressure On Me	What Can Be Done To Lessen The Pressure
Grades		
Classmates		
Teachers		
Homework		
Preparation for the future		
Extra-curricular activities		
Other		

Family

People scoring high on this scale tend to experience stress related to their family. This stress may be related to family hardships, deaths in the family, divorce, financial problems, and arguments. The following exercises are designed to help you explore the pressures you experience related to your family life. (use name codes)

What is most stressful for you at home?

_____
_____
_____
_____
_____

How much control do you have over this situation? What could you change?

_____
_____
_____
_____
_____

What else causes you stress at home?

_____
_____
_____
_____
_____

What can you do to make these situations better?

_____
_____
_____
_____
_____

Family Pressure

Complete this chart to identify your pressures. (Use name codes.)

Type of Pressure	Who Is Putting This Pressure On Me	What Can Be Done To Lessen The Pressure
Illness or addiction		
Finances		
Family or step-family		
Divorce or separation		
Arguments		
Discipline		
Death		
Other		

Personal

People scoring high on this scale tend to experience stress related to their personal life. This stress may be related to your physical appearance, changing schools, a new job, risky behavior and/or getting into trouble with the police. The following exercises are designed to help you explore the pressures you experience related to your personal life.

Which personal situation do you wish was different?

_____

_____

_____

In what ways is it under your control to change it? What would you change?

_____

_____

_____

How could you change it?

_____

_____

_____

What other personal situations would you like to change?

_____

_____

_____

How are you able to?

_____

_____

_____

Personal Pressure

Complete this chart to identify your pressures. Use name codes.

Type Of Pressure	Who Is Putting This Pressure On Me	What Can Be Done To Alleviate The Pressure
Illness or Addiction		
My Appearance/ My Body		
Getting into Trouble		
Sexual Issues		
Having Too Much to Do		
Moving Away		
Other		

Social

People scoring high on this scale tend to experience stress related to social life. This stress may be related to dating issues, pressure to do things you do not want to do, experiencing loss, and changes in your social status. The following exercises are designed to help you explore the pressures you experience related to school.

Which of your social situations would you like to be different?

_____

_____

_____

_____

_____

In what ways is it under your control to change it? What would you change?

_____

_____

_____

_____

_____

What other social situation would you like to be different?

_____

_____

_____

_____

_____

In what ways is it under your control to change it? What would you change?

_____

_____

_____

_____

_____

Social Pressure

Complete this chart to identify your pressures. (Use name codes.)

Type of Pressure	Who is Putting This Pressure on Me	What can be Done to Lessen the Pressure
Peer-pressure to take drugs		
Peer-pressure to drink alcohol		
A loss		
Pressure to join a gang		
Pressure to dress differently		
Dating issues		
Other		

   © 2012 WHOLE PERSON ASSOCIATES, 101 W. 2nd ST., SUITE 203, DULUTH MN 55802 • 800-247-6789

The Problem-Solving Process

After you have identified the primary sources of your stress, develop a plan for solving the problem. Sometimes this plan will be to change your behavior (being more assertive when pressured to wear a different style of clothes), or the plan might be to take action to reduce the stress you are feeling (begin meditating before bed).

The problem-solving process is a search for, and implementation of, the best possible solution to your stress problem. The following is an example of a problem-solving process:

STEP 1 – Define the problem to see the situation as it really is.
You can do so by answering these questions:

What is causing the problem? _____

_____

Where is it occurring? _____

_____

How is it occurring? _____

_____

When is it occurring? _____

_____

With whom is it occurring? _____

_____

Why is it occurring? _____

_____

What is my role in the problem? _____

_____

What have I tried to resolve the situation? _____

_____

(Continued on the next page)

The Problem-Solving Process *(Continued)*

Step 2 – Consider all possibilities by brainstorming possible solutions to the problem. You can do so by answering these questions:

What other ways can I look at the problem? _____

_____

What can I control in the situation? _____

_____

What can I not control in the situation? _____

_____

What are some possible ways to approach the problem? _____

_____

Step 3 – Weigh the consequences of courses of action to resolve the problem. You can do so by answering these questions:

What are the pros of each option? _____

_____

What are the cons of each option? _____

_____

What are the logical consequences of each option? _____

_____

How does each option apply equally to each person involved? _____

_____

(Continued on the next page)

The Problem-Solving Process *(Continued)*

Step 4 – Weigh the alternatives to each course of action.
You can do so by answering these questions:

Which option best fits my situation?_____

_____

How will the other people involved in the situation be affected?_____

_____

How will each alternative contribute to harmony for all people involved?_____

_____

How will this reduce the amount of stress in my life?_____

_____

Step 5 – Make a final decision.

Step 6 – Act on your decision.

What is the best way to begin taking action?_____

_____

_____

_____

_____

Step 7 – Evaluate whether the problem has been resolved or not.

_____

_____

_____

_____

_____

Sources of Stress Quotations

These quotes are related to how people view stress. Select one that speaks to you directly and write a short description about something that happened in your life related to the quote.

❑ *Sometimes the most important thing in a whole day is the rest we take between two deep breaths.* ~ **Etty Hillesum**

❑ *Is everything as urgent as your stress would imply?* ~ **Carrie Latet**

❑ *In times of stress, be bold and valiant.* ~ **Horace**

_____

_____

_____

_____

_____

_____

_____

_____

_____

_____

_____

_____

_____

_____

_____

_____

_____

_____

_____

_____

_____

© 2012 WHOLE PERSON ASSOCIATES, 101 W. 2nd ST., SUITE 203, DULUTH MN 55802 ▪ 800-247-6789

My Greatest Sources of Stress

Use name codes.

Journal about what you believe to be your greatest source of stress at school.

_____

_____

_____

_____

_____

Journal about what you believe to be your greatest source of stress in your family life.

_____

_____

_____

_____

_____

Journal about what you believe to be your greatest source of stress in your personal life.

_____

_____

_____

_____

_____

Journal about what you believe to be your greatest source of stress in your social life.

_____

_____

_____

_____

_____

Teenage Stress Factors

- Academic pressure

- Decisions about what to do after graduation

- Career Decisions

- Adaptation to bodily changes

- Family conflicts

- Peer conflicts

- Pressure to do, dress and act in ways you don't want

- Pressure to fit in

- Taking on too many activities

- Social life

- Dating issues

- Friendships

- Gender/cultural/disability issues

Types of Stress

- Short-term stress that arises when you need motivation and inspiration. It will increase your performance before athletic competitions, creative projects, and challenging tasks.

- Negative stress due to constant changes in your routine. These changes cause feelings of uneasiness, unfamiliarity and discomfort. This stress usually lasts a long time.

- Stress that occurs when you are pushed beyond your limits by being overloaded with too many things to do.

- Stress that occurs when you are bored and restless, and need to be challenged.

SECTION III:
Social Media Safety Scale

Name_____

Date_____

Eustress vs. Distress Directions

Stress is a burst of energy, telling our body what to do. Eustress is another name for good stress, which is the helpful type of stress. Eustress becomes distress when it is overdone. It is the type of stress that can help you accomplish good things in your life. It can be a factor, motivating us to move forward and enjoy events and accomplish actions that require some effort but provide satisfaction. Eustress can help you accomplish tasks, goals, and projects. The secret, however, is to plan for this good stress, and to learn to change from experiencing distress to eustress. The *Eustress vs. Distress Scale* is designed to help you identify how well you set yourself up to experience good stress in your life.

This scale contains 32 statements divided into four sections. Read each statement and decide how close the statement is with your beliefs about yourself and about the world.

Circle 3 if you agree with the statement

Circle 2 if the statement may be true for you

Circle 1 if you disagree with the statement

3 = Agree   2 = Maybe   1 = Disagree

I. CHALLENGE

I believe it is natural for things to change. 3   (2)   1

In the above statement, the circled 2 means that the statement may be true for the test taker. Ignore the TOTAL lines below each section. They are for scoring purposes and will be used later.

This is not a test and there are no right or wrong answers. Do not spend too much time thinking about your answers. Your initial response will be the most true for you.
Be sure to respond to every statement.

(Turn to the next page and begin)

Eustress vs. Distress Scale

3 = Agree   2 = Maybe   1 = Disagree

I. CHALLENGE

I believe it is natural for things to change 3   2   1

I see change as an opportunity for better things to come 3   2   1

I thrive under conditions of difficulty and adversity 3   2   1

I can turn change into opportunity 3   2   1

I am able to rise to the occasion in stressful situations 3   2   1

I view stress as lessons to learn in life 3   2   1

I see stressful events as necessary for personal growth 3   2   1

I view problems as challenges 3   2   1

TOTAL = _____

II. OPTIMISM

I remain hopeful regardless of what happens 3   2   1

I am usually optimistic about my future 3   2   1

I remain positive even when things do not go my way 3   2   1

I look at the bright side of things 3   2   1

I am happy most of the time 3   2   1

I usually smile and I am pleasant to be around 3   2   1

I see the glass half full, not half empty 3   2   1

I usually maintain a positive attitude 3   2   1

TOTAL = _____

(Continued on the next page)

(Eustress vs. Distress Scale continued)

3 = Agree   2 = Maybe   1 = Disagree

III. CONTROL

I believe I can influence events in my life.	3	2	1
I am aware of my reactions to events in my life.	3	2	1
I think about how to turn difficult situations into opportunities	3	2	1
I set goals and work toward them	3	2	1
I rarely give up on a challenge.	3	2	1
I try not to stress about things I cannot control.	3	2	1
I can control negative thoughts during times of stress	3	2	1
I react optimistically to transitions in my life	3	2	1

TOTAL = _____

IV. FOCUS

I focus my energy when I need to	3	2	1
I set goals and work to achieve them	3	2	1
I can motivate myself.	3	2	1
I have a positive vision of what is possible	3	2	1
I never give up until tasks are completed	3	2	1
I stay calm and focused under pressure.	3	2	1
I rarely worry about what others say about me	3	2	1
I develop a plan when given a big task to complete	3	2	1

TOTAL = _____

(Go to the Scoring Directions on the next page)

Eustress vs. Distress Scale
Scoring Directions

Even though stress may not always be comfortable for you, it is not always a bad thing if you experience it in moderate amounts and don't let it control you. In fact, stress can be very beneficial in helping you deal with challenges and difficult situations. While a lot of stress can be destructive, a little bit of stress can help you to be prepared, work harder and perform your best. It can stimulate you. The secret is to view challenges as opportunities, maintain a positive attitude, try to control only what you can, and plan for success.

To score the scale you just completed, add the numbers you have circled for each of the four sections on the previous pages. Put that total on the line marked TOTAL at the end of each section.

Then, transfer your totals for each of the four sections to the spaces below:

CHALLENGE TOTAL = _____

OPTIMISM TOTAL　 = _____

CONTROL TOTAL　 = _____

FOCUS TOTAL　　 = _____

Profile Interpretation

Individual Scales Scores	Result	Indications
19 to 24	high	If you score high on any of the scales, it indicates that you have been able to develop stress management skills in those areas.
14 to 18	moderate	If you score moderate on any of the scales, it indicates that you have been able to develop some stress management skills in those areas, but still need additional assistance.
8 to 13	low	If you score low on any of the scales, it indicates that you need to take a more active role in developing stress management skills in those areas.

The following pages contain ideas and activities for you to complete in order to help you experience more good stress.

Upcoming Challenges

Challenge is defined as the ability to view life changes and potential stressful situations as opportunities rather than threats. Challenge relates to your ability to effectively manage stress. People who are able to perceive stressful situations as opportunities will experience good stress. They are able to positively view the challenges of a stressful situation and even look at it as a learning experience. They see themselves as having many different options in these types of situations. (Use name codes.)

My Upcoming Challenges	Stress I Associate With These Challenges	How I Can Look At Them As Opportunities
Ex: I have to give a speech in English class.	*I'm afraid I'll be so nervous that I'll forget what I have to say and everyone will laugh.*	*This is a chance to see how I do at public speaking. Even if I don't do too well, it's practice for the future.*

My Challenge

Choose one of your upcoming challenges that you are feeling particularly stressed about. This challenge may be competing in a sports event, going on a date, making a major purchase, speaking in public or looking for a job.

What is your challenge?

_____

_____

_____

_____

_____

What about this challenge is stressing you?

_____

_____

_____

_____

_____

How can this challenge be viewed as an opportunity?

_____

_____

_____

_____

_____

What can you gain from this challenge?

_____

_____

_____

_____

_____

Maintaining Optimism

Optimism is defined as your ability to maintain a positive world-view. Optimism is seeing the glass as half full rather than half empty. People displaying an optimistic world-view, regardless of setbacks and disappointments, look at the bright side of things and see the possibilities that challenging situations offer.

My Upcoming Challenges	Stress Associated with these Challenges	How I Can Perceive them Optimistically
Ex: Public speaking in my English class	Fear of making a fool of myself	I'll do the best I can and assume people will understand.

Optimism in My Situation

Thinking about one of the challenges you have been writing about, respond to the following questions:

What negative thoughts come into your head about the challenge?

_____

_____

_____

_____

_____

How can you turn these negative thoughts into more positive ones?

_____

_____

_____

_____

_____

What skills do you possess that will help you in this situation?

_____

_____

_____

_____

_____

What positive qualities do you possess that will help you in this situation?

_____

_____

_____

_____

_____

In Control

Being in control is defined as the belief that an individual has influence over his or her life. Resilient people are able to identify situations in which they do and do not have control. They tend to control their thoughts about the stress they are encountering, their feelings about the situation, how they behave, and their choices. It is the firm belief that they can influence how they will react and the willingness to act on that belief.

My Upcoming Challenges	Things I Can't Control about the Situation	Things I Can Control about the Situation
Ex: Speaking in front of my English class	*How others react to my speech*	*How hard I prepare and how I behave afterward, no matter what anyone says.*

Control in My Situation

Think about the challenge you have been writing about. What will help you gain control in this situation?

_____
_____
_____

Learning to relax is one way of controlling stress. What are some different ways that you can relax more?

_____
_____
_____

What choices can you make to gain more control in the situation?

_____
_____
_____

What thoughts can you control to ensure success in the situation?

_____
_____
_____

Read the Serenity Prayer:

God grant me the serenity
to accept the things I cannot change;
courage to change the things I can;
and wisdom to know the difference.

Is this a situation you can control? _____

_____
_____

Focusing My Energy

People who are resilient are able to stay focused on the task at hand. They do not allow other interests and other people dissuade them from their goal. They know various ways to support the success of their work. They make the task at hand their first priority and take responsibility for achieving it successfully.

My Upcoming Challenges	How I Have Trouble Staying Focused	How I Can Focus My Energies
Ex: Speaking in front of my English class	I try to avoid thinking about it.	Write an outline of my speech to help organize my thoughts.

Focus on Setting Goals

By developing a plan and identifying activities related to the challenge, you create your own motivation, rather than relying on other circumstances. Now, set purposeful goals to help you maintain your motivation.

Select one of your upcoming challenges: _____

_____

Example: I am giving a speech in English class and want it to be thorough and smooth.

Write a list of actions that you will take to keep you focused and that will help you to achieve your goal.

Example: I will research the topic, look up info on the internet and go to the library. When I'm done writing it, I will rehearse it several times in front of my mirror.

Action #1: _____

_____

_____

Action #2: _____

_____

_____

Action #3: _____

_____

_____

Action #4: _____

_____

_____

How can you focus on these actions and not let other things distract you?

_____

_____

_____

(Continued on the next page)

Focus on Setting Goals *(Continued)*

Keeping your challenge in mind, who can you avoid to make the challenge your priority?

_____

_____

_____

_____

What can you avoid to make the challenge your priority?

_____

_____

_____

_____

Who can help you?

_____

_____

_____

_____

What distracts you from meeting important challenges?

_____

_____

_____

_____

How will you know when you are ready to meet the challenge?
How do you think you will feel?

_____

_____

_____

_____

Putting it All Together

It is time to put your plan together to ensure that you experience EUSTRESS (good stress) as opposed to DISTRESS (bad stress). This will help you to develop good stress by building resiliency through the four steps you just learned. For this activity, pull all of the information together that you just completed, to develop a plan for successfully meeting an upcoming challenge.

Your upcoming challenge _____

Steps to Success	What I Will Do	How it Will Help Me
Challenge		
Optimism		
Control		
Focus		
Other		
Other		

Eustress

How can good stress help me?

_____

_____

_____

_____

_____

_____

_____

_____

_____

_____

_____

_____

What will I do to be sure I experience more eustress (good stress)?

_____

_____

_____

_____

_____

_____

_____

_____

_____

_____

_____

_____

Good Stress Quotations

Choose two quotations below. On the lines that follow each of them, describe what each of the quotes means to you and how it relates to your ability to listen for meaning.

Stress is an ignorant state. It believes that everything is an emergency.
> **~ Natalie Goldberg**

_____

_____

_____

_____

_____

_____

There cannot be a stressful crisis next week. My schedule is already full.
> **~ Henry Kissinger**

_____

_____

_____

_____

_____

_____

Stress is when you wake up screaming and you realize you haven't fallen asleep yet.
> **~ Anonymous**

_____

_____

_____

_____

_____

_____

Characteristics of Distress

- Can be short or long term

- Exists outside of our coping abilities

- Feels unpleasant

- Decreases performance

- Can lead to mental issues

- Can lead to physical problems

- Causes anxiety

- Can lead to over-commitment

- Reflects chronic urgency

- Builds impatience

- Prevents ability to relax without feeling guilty

- Feels like no time

Characteristics of Eustress

- Focuses on energy

- Motivates

- Feels exciting

- Is necessary for gaining top results

- Improves performance

- Allows you to plan and work toward your goals

- Tells your body when you need to act

- Helps you make changes in your life

- Can be healthy

- Provides and energy boost

- Helps you to cope

- Helps you to develop the courage to take positive risks

- Leads to racing heart, flutter in stomach, and sparkle in eyes.

Examples of Eustress (Good Stress)

- Loving watching the ocean waves or surfing is eustress. When that same ocean becomes a tsunami, that is distress.

- Joining the choir and performing is eustress. Taking on other obligations as well, along with homework, is distress.

- Eustress is …

    Riding a roller-coaster

    Weight training

    Meeting a challenge

    Coming in first place

    Watching a suspenseful movie

    Stepping up to make a foul shot

    Getting ready to go to a big dance

    Looking forward to your birthday

    Receiving a call or text from an old friend

    Having your team win

    Celebrating the holidays

    Looking forward to vacation

SECTION IV:
Stressed for Success Scale

Name_____

Date_____

Stressed for Success Scale
Directions

Pressure to succeed can be very stressful. Whether you are getting pressure from your parents, family, caregivers, friends, teachers, or yourself, this pressure can produce distress.

The *Stressed for Success Scale* is designed to help you identify the types of pressure you are feeling. This scale contains 24 statements that are divided into four categories. Read each of the statements and decide how descriptive the statement is of you. In each of the choices listed, circle the number of your response on the line to the right of each statement.

In the following example, the circled 1 indicates the statement is not at all descriptive of the person completing the scale.

4 = Very Descriptive   **3 = Somewhat Descriptive**   **2 = A Little Descriptive**   **1 = Not At All Descriptive**

In school . . .

I have trouble completing assignments on time   4   3   2   (1)

This is not a test and there are no right or wrong answers. Do not spend too much time thinking about your answers. Your initial response will be the most true for you.
Be sure to respond to every statement.

(Turn to the next page and begin)

Stressed for Success Scale

4 = Very Descriptive   **3 = Somewhat Descriptive**   **2 = A Little Descriptive**   **1 = Not At All Descriptive**

In school . . .

I have trouble completing assignments on time	4	3	2	1
The demands of school are too much for me at times	4	3	2	1
I have trouble getting my homework done	4	3	2	1
It's difficult for me to focus when I study	4	3	2	1
I have to cheat to get good grades	4	3	2	1
I often miss deadlines	4	3	2	1

A - TOTAL = _____

When it comes to school and extra-curricular activities . . .

I am involved all of my extra time	4	3	2	1
I can't seem to get everything done	4	3	2	1
I overextend myself by belonging to a lot of clubs	4	3	2	1
I overextend myself by playing too many sports	4	3	2	1
I have many options and I want to do them all	4	3	2	1
I can't say no	4	3	2	1

O - TOTAL = _____

(Continued on the next page)

(Stressed for Success Scale continued)

4 = Very Descriptive	3 = Somewhat Descriptive	2 = A Little Descriptive	1 = Not At All Descriptive

When is a lot expected of me, by myself or others . . .

My teachers have high expectations of me 4   3   2   1

My parents/caregivers want me to get very good grades 4   3   2   1

I am obsessed with getting good grades 4   3   2   1

My parents/caregivers expect a lot of me 4   3   2   1

My friends expect me to succeed 4   3   2   1

I feel I must meet my parent's expectations 4   3   2   1

E - TOTAL = _____

When it comes to my future . . .

I wonder if I can afford further education 4   3   2   1

I worry about competing for jobs 4   3   2   1

I want to make a lot of money 4   3   2   1

I need to get into a good college 4   3   2   1

I'm concerned because I don't know what kind of work
I want to do or can do 4   3   2   1

I don't know what I want to do with my life 4   3   2   1

F - TOTAL = _____

(Go to the Scoring Directions on the next page)

Stressed for Success Scale
Scoring Directions

All teens feel a certain amount of pressure to succeed. For some, this stress is greater than for others. The *Stressed for Success Scale* is designed to measure the amount of stress you are experiencing to achieve success. For each of the four sections on the previous pages, count the scores you circled for each of the four sections. Put that total on the line marked "Total" at the end of each section.

Then, transfer your totals to the spaces below:

A - ACADEMICS TOTAL = _____

O - OVER-EXTENDING TOTAL = _____

E - EXPECTATIONS TOTAL = _____

F - FUTURE TOTAL = _____

Profile Interpretation

Individual Scales Scores	Result	Indications
19 to 24	high	Scores from 19 to 24 on any of the above scale are HIGH and indicate that you have a great deal of pressure to succeed in those areas.
12 to 18	moderate	Scores from 12 to 18 on any of the above scales are MODERATE and indicate that you have some pressure to succeed in those areas.
6 to 11	low	Scores from 6 to 11 on any of the above scales are LOW and indicate that you do not have pressure to succeed in those areas.

No matter how you scored, low, moderate or high, you will benefit from the exercises that follow.

Academics

In the following charts identify the people who pressure you in your academics – positively and negatively – how they do it, and how it helps or hurts you. You can leave either the third or fourth column blank. If this person's pressure hurts AND helps, fill them both in.

Person (name code)	How this person pressures me	How does it help me?	How does it hurt me?

Things I Do Well In School

Identify those things you do well and then what you need to improve in school. In the table that follows, identify those things that you do well when in school.

School Activities	Things I Do Well
Ex: Study	*Study in a room with no distractions, even shut my cell phone off. I keep everything organized and manage my time well.*
Study	
Write	
Read	
Research	
Homework	
Time Management	
Clubs/Organizations	
Sports	
Other	

© 2012 WHOLE PERSON ASSOCIATES, 101 W. 2nd ST., SUITE 203, DULUTH MN 55802 ▪ 800-247-6789

Things I Do Not Do Well in School

Now that you know what you do well, it is time to look at those areas that you could improve. In the table that follows, identify those things that you do not do well when in school.

School Activities	Things I Could Improve
Ex: Study	*I keep the TV on, answer my texts (I hate to miss anything) and I wait till the very last minute.*
Study	
Write	
Read	
Research	
Homework	
Time Management	
Clubs/Organizations	
Sports	
Other	

Over-Extending

People scoring high on this scale tend to have pressure to do it all. They feel pressured to get involved in a variety of activities. In the following charts identify the people who pressure you – positively and negatively – how they do it, and how it helps or hurts you. You can leave either the third or fourth column blank. If this person's pressure hurts AND helps, fill them both in.

Person (name code)	How this person pressures me to do more than I am already doing	How does it help me?	How does it hurt me?

My Activities

In the chart that follows, list all of the activities you are involved in and complete the rest of the table.

My Activities	What I Do	Amount of Time I Spend Per Week
Clubs and/or organizations (Chess, Religion, etc.)		
Music in which I participate		
Volunteering / Jobs		
Sports I play or watch		
Other		
Other		

With which activities are you spending too much time? _____

_____

_____

High Expectations

People scoring high on this scale tend to feel pressure from high expectations to do well and succeed at all costs. In the following charts identify the people who pressure you positively and negatively, how they do it, and how it helps or hurts you. You can leave either the third or fourth column blank. If this person's pressure hurts AND helps, fill them both in.

Person (name code)	How this person pressures me with high expectations	How does it help me?	How does it hurt me?

Expectations on Me

Complete the following sentences-starters about your expectations of yourself and those of others in your life and then check whether you perceive these expectations to be realistic or unrealistic.

I put expectations on myself to _____

_____

_____ ❑ realistic ❑ unrealistic

My parents/caregivers expect me to _____

_____

_____ ❑ realistic ❑ unrealistic

My teacher _____ (name code) expects _____

_____

_____ ❑ realistic ❑ unrealistic

I put expectations on myself to _____

_____

_____ ❑ realistic ❑ unrealistic

My coaches, tutors or trainers (name code) _____expect me to _____

_____

_____ ❑ realistic ❑ unrealistic

Another adult _____ (name code) expects me to _____

_____

_____ ❑ realistic ❑ unrealistic

One of my peers (name code) _____ expect me to _____

_____

_____ ❑ realistic ❑ unrealistic

My family member (name code) _____ expects me _____

_____

_____ ❑ realistic ❑ unrealistic

Future

People scoring high on this scale tend to have pressure on them to make decisions for the future. In the following table identify the people who pressure you positively and negatively, how they do it, and how it helps or hurts you. You can leave either the third or fourth column blank. If this person's pressure hurts AND helps, fill them both in.

Person (name code)	How this person pressures me to make decisions about my future	How does it help me?	How does it hurt me?

I'm Worried

Teens worry about their future. By exploring what you are concerned or worried about, you can reduce your stress associated with those concerns.

My worries about my future	What I can do to reduce this worry
Finished with School – *Ex: What happens when I'm done with school? Will I get a job? What kind?*	*I'll think about my interests and what I like to do and talk with the school counselor.*
Finished with School	
Further Education	
Family	
Friends	
Dating	
Finances	
Other	
Other	

My Work/Career Future

My job/career interests are _____

_____

_____

_____

My skills are _____

_____

_____

_____

My ideal job(s) that would combine my interests and skills are _____

_____

_____

_____

The kind of education or training that is needed for my ideal job(s) is _____

_____

_____

_____

I can investigate which trade school or college specializes in my ideal job by _____

_____

_____

_____

Perhaps I can volunteer at _____

_____

_____ to help me figure out if I like the work or environment.

Perhaps I can get a part time job at _____

_____

_____ to help me figure out if I like the work or environment.

Future Preparation

How prepared are you for the future?

What I Need to Do to Prepare for the Future	How I Will Prepare
Respectful Attitude	
Responsible Behavior	
Knowledge of How to Manage Money	
Basic Writing Skills	
Basic Math Skills	
Involvement in the Community	
Time Management Skills	

Pressure to Succeed Quotations

Journal your thoughts about this quotation and how it pertains to you, and perhaps to someone you know.

All pressure is self-inflicted. It's what you make of it or how you let it rub off on you.
~ Sebastian Coe

_____

_____

_____

_____

_____

_____

_____

_____

_____

_____

_____

_____

_____

_____

_____

_____

_____

_____

_____

_____

_____

_____

My Thoughts

Journal your thoughts on the following:

Academics _____

_____

_____

_____

_____

_____

_____

Over-Extending _____

_____

_____

_____

_____

_____

_____

Expectations _____

_____

_____

_____

_____

_____

_____

Future _____

_____

_____

_____

_____

_____

_____

Ineffective Responses to Pressure

- cry, yell, pout
- say "It's none of your business"
- slam doors
- hang up the telephone
- say something sarcastic or mean
- say you'll do it and then don't
- walk away and ignore the person

Effective Responses to Pressure

- use direct eye contact
- keep confident and assertive body language
- ask for the right time to talk
- stay calm
- explain why this is not what you see in your future
- give a good reason why it's a bad idea
- say "Thanks, but no thanks"
- ask for help about how to achieve this goal
- say you'll consider it and will think about it

Ways to Overcome Pressure to Succeed

- Change negative thoughts to positive ones

- Prioritize your activities

- Continually question the negative views you have of yourself

- Manage your time constructively

- Don't be so hard on yourself

- Set realistic and attainable goals

- Stop comparing yourself to others

- Give yourself positive affirmations and self-talk

- Continue to develop your strengths

SECTION V:
How I Deal with My Stress Scale

Name_____

Date_____

How I Deal with My Stress Scale
Directions

Your body's natural reaction to challenging events that seem to feel overwhelming is fight or flight. This fight or flight reaction causes a faster heart rate, shallow breathing and a desire to flee. However, you can teach yourself to perceive events to be within your control and you can even change your body reactions to challenging events.

This scale will help you identify how you have been dealing with stress in your life.

In the following example, the circled numbers indicate how much the statement is descriptive of the person completing the inventory.

	Very Often	Often	Sometimes	Never
When I am in a stressful situation, I deal with my stress by . . .				
doing activities that help me relax	4	(3)	2	1

This is not a test and there are no right or wrong answers. Do not spend too much time thinking about your answers. Your initial response will be the most true for you.
Be sure to respond to every statement.

(Turn to the next page and begin)

How I Deal with My Stress Scale

	Very Often	Often	Sometimes	Never

When I am in a stressful situation, I deal with my stress by . . .

	Very Often	Often	Sometimes	Never
doing activities that help me relax	4	3	2	1
trying to let my body relax	4	3	2	1
overeating	1	2	3	4
using unhealthy drugs	1	2	3	4
watching a funny movie or television show	4	3	2	1
behaving in an unhealthy, risky way	1	2	3	4
drinking alcohol or smoking	1	2	3	4
yelling at others	1	2	3	4
listening to calming music	4	3	2	1
resting for short periods of time	4	3	2	1
finding others to blame	1	2	3	4
doing something physical	4	3	2	1
talking to someone who is supportive	4	3	2	1
breaking things	1	2	3	4
playing sports	4	3	2	1
verbally attacking others	1	2	3	4
getting into fights	1	2	3	4
denying that I am stressed or upset	1	2	3	4
letting my feelings out constructively	4	3	2	1
slowing down my breathing	4	3	2	1

TOTAL # 1 = _____

(Continued on the next page)

(How I Deal with My Stress Scale continued)

	Very Often	Often	Sometimes	Never
When I am in a stressful situation, I deal with my stress by . . .				
hurting myself physically	1	2	3	4
sleeping a lot	1	2	3	4
thinking in a positive way	4	3	2	1
trying to change things that I have no control over	1	2	3	4
pretending it will go away	1	2	3	4
looking for comfort with my spirituality/religion	4	3	2	1
hanging out with people I care about	4	3	2	1
exercising regularly	4	3	2	1
eating nutritiously	4	3	2	1
stopping my negative self talk	4	3	2	1
trying to be perfect	1	2	3	4
practicing deep breathing	4	3	2	1
reading inspirational books	4	3	2	1
doing something positive for others	4	3	2	1
bullying others	1	2	3	4
lowering my unrealistic expectations	4	3	2	1
dwelling on my weaknesses	1	2	3	4
thinking about hurting myself	1	2	3	4
making time for fun	4	3	2	1
getting depressed	1	2	3	4

TOTAL # 2 = _____

(Go to the Scoring Directions on the next page)

How I Deal with My Stress Scale
Scoring Directions

The *How I Deal with My Stress Scale* is designed to measure the strength of your ability to deal with stress in your life. For each of the sections on the previous pages, count the scores you circled for each of the two sections. Put that total on the line marked TOTAL at the end of each section.

Then, transfer your totals to the spaces below:

TOTAL # 1 = _____

TOTAL # 2 = _____

Add these two scores (you will get a number from 40-160) to get your grand total and put that number below:

GRAND TOTAL = _____

Profile Interpretation

Grand Total	Result	Indications
121 to 160	high	If you score high, you are dealing with stress very effectively.
80 to 120	moderate	If you score moderate, you are dealing with stress fairly effectively.
40 to 79	low	If you score low, you significantly need to improve your stress management.

When you are not able to cope with the stress that you encounter in your life, you begin to feel tension and frustration. The following exercises will help you learn to change your reactions during times of stress.

My Helping Skills

You have many skills that would be useful in helping others. List what you consider your primary skills and identify how you could use these skills to help others.

My Skills	How Can I Help Others or Volunteer Using These Skills
School work – *Ex: Writing*	*Go to a skilled-care facility and offer to write notes or letters dictated by some of the residents who cannot do their own writing.*
School work	
Arts	
Music	
Sports	
Cooking/Baking	
Mechanical	
Technology	
Other	

Unrealistic Expectations

Try lowering your expectations.

What expectations do you have about yourself that may be unrealistic?

Unrealistic Expectations I Have of Myself	How Can I Lower These Expectations

What unrealistic expectations do you have of others? Use name code.

Person	My Expectations Are . . .	In What Ways Is This Expectation Realistic or Unrealistic?

Set Realistic Goals

What are some of your goals?
Identify goals below and the steps you can take to reach these goals.

Areas of My Life	Goals	Steps to Reach the Goal
Friendships	*Not to be so possessive of my friends or dating friends.*	*I will try to notice my behavior with a new friend. I am asking too much of them I need to stop.*
Friendships		
School		
Extra Curricular Activities		
Family		
Others		
Others		

What Goes Through My Head?

Feelings of stress are definitely influenced by your thoughts and perceptions. Stress is often how you react to an event and what you say to yourself. Think back to times when you were stressed. Write the events you thought about and how you felt, to become more aware of your feelings. Use name codes.

Your Stress Producing Situation	Thoughts that Go Through Your Head	How You Felt When This Situation Happened	How has this Situation been Resolved?
Ex: GRW is moving to another city.	She won't be my best friend anymore. We'll lose contact. She'll find another best friend. I won't be able to.	When I found out, I was devastated.	We still are good friends. We email every day. We've both found other best friends in our school.

If you see trends, what are they? _____

_____

_____

Adding Physical Activities

Adding physical activities to your schedule will help reduce stress.
What types of physical activities appeal to you?

_____

_____

Take Breaks

Sometimes you may need to break away from what is causing you stress and do things you enjoy. Some of these activities might include reading books, watching movies, or walking your dog. What type of breaks can you take when you are feeling stressed?

_____

_____

_____

Recognize Triggers

What or who triggers your stress? Use Name codes.

Triggers	Why this Causes Stress
Ex: When BSU keeps asking about my getting a part-time job.	*Since I have so many friends and activities, I don't want to give any of them up, even though I know we need the extra money.*

Worry Journal

Keep a journal to write about the worries and stressors in your life. By doing this, you will be able to identify the stress, acknowledge it as part of your life, and begin to deal with the stress. You may want to put your journal entries in a Problem Solving Box and set a specific time each day or week to focus on letting go of what you cannot control and search for solutions for ones you can control.

Some examples of teen worries: school grades, appearance, popularity, health, bullying or being bullied, school violence, divorce in a family, dating, friendships and lack of them, drugs and drinking, hunger and poverty, nuclear bombs, terrorist attacks, etc.

Journal Entries	This is Worrying Me or Causing Me Stress
Journal Entry 1	
Journal Entry 2	
Journal Entry 3	
Journal Entry 4	
Journal Entry 5	
Journal Entry 6	
Journal Entry 7	

Plan Your Time

Planning your time can help you reduce stress. When you have no idea of what you need to do and when you do not have a plan of ways to get it done, you will feel stressed. In the table below, write out a list of things you need to do next week and what you need to do before to be prepared.

Days of the Week	What I Need to Do Before	How I Can Get This Done
Monday	Ex: I have an English test tomorrow. I need to help BLJ with her homework today, I have choir practice and need to be home at 6 for dinner. I want to go out with my friends tonight.	I will put my choir notebook in my backpack. Tell BLJ I'll meet her at 4 for an hour. Choir practice for an hour and home to study. I'll see friends on another night.
Tuesday		
Wednesday		
Thursday		
Friday		
Saturday		
Sunday		

Who Can I Talk To?

You can reduce your stress by talking about your issues with other people you trust and respect (parents, siblings, friends, teachers, etc.) In the spaces below, list those people (use name codes) who will support you in times of stress and then list why you chose them.

Person	Why this Person Would Be Good to Talk With

© 2012 WHOLE PERSON ASSOCIATES, 101 W. 2nd ST., SUITE 203, DULUTH MN 55802 • 800-247-6789

Changes in My Wellness Habits

By taking better care of yourself, you can reduce feelings of stress. Think about your eating, sleeping and exercising habits. In the table that follows, write about how you can make positive change in your wellness habits.

Wellness Habits	How I Can Change in a Positive Way
Eating	*Ex: At lunch I'll get a salad rather than French fries.*
Drinking	
Exercising	
Sleeping	
Spirituality	
Other	

What types of changes are you willing to make immediately to begin reducing stress in your life?

_____

_____

_____

_____

My Strengths

You can reduce stress by accepting yourself and identifying your unique strengths and building on them. What are your strengths and how could you use these strengths? Complete the sentence starters below that relate to you.

I show my creativity by _____

I can use this strength by _____

My athleticism is _____

I can use this strength by _____

I like to work with my hands by_____

I can use this strength by _____

I am like this animal _____ because _____

I can use this strength by _____

I like to _____ with my computer.

I can use this strength by _____

Math and I are _____

I can use this strength by _____

I write when _____

I can use this strength by _____

When I need to speak in front of the class I _____

I can use this strength by _____

I excel in _____

I can use this strength by _____

I am great in _____

I can use this strength by _____

I am an excellent _____

I can use this strength by _____

What are your greatest strengths?

_____

_____

_____

Learning to Say "NO"

Many people find themselves trying to do too much, and usually in too short of time. This stresses them out. You may need to find a good balance by decreasing the commitments of when you have a choice. Below, identify those activities you want to keep and why, and those you do not want to keep.

Activities I Want to Keep	Why I Like These Activities

Activities I Feel I Can Let Go	Why?

Sources of Stress Quotes

The quote that follows is related to how people view stress. Think about it and then complete the question prompts.

Stress is not what happens to us. It's our response to what happens. And response is something we can choose.
~ Maureen Killoran

It seems that I get most stressed about . . .

_____

_____

_____

_____

_____

_____

I can begin looking at challenging situations as less stressful by . . .

_____

_____

_____

_____

_____

_____

I will respond to distress by . . .

_____

_____

_____

_____

_____

_____

My Stress Relievers

Journal about three of the stress-reduction techniques you like and make a commitment to use.

_____

_____

_____

_____

_____

_____

_____

_____

_____

_____

_____

_____

_____

Sign with your name code _____

Journal about three of the stress-reduction techniques you do not like and will not work for you and why.

_____

_____

_____

_____

_____

_____

_____

_____

_____

_____

_____

_____

A Healthy Stress Mind-Set

- Think positively in challenging situations
- Have a support system and ask for their help
- Participate in activities for fun
- Believe that setbacks are temporary
- Acknowledge that there will be some things you cannot control
- Believe that you will succeed if you keep working toward your goals

Unhealthy Ways of Coping with Stress

- Take your stress out on others by yelling, angry outbursts, bullying
- Keep busy every moment to avoid facing problems
- Procrastinate
- Use pills, drugs or alcoholic drinks to relax
- Sleeping too much
- Over or under eating
- Sitting for hours in front of the TV, computer, etc.
- Withdrawing from friends and family
- Overdoing computer games, texting, etc.
- Discontinuing usual activities